G. I. F. T. E. D.
(Guiding Ideals For True, Enduring, and Devoted)
Love

G. I. F. T. E. D.
***(Guiding Ideals For True, Enduring, and Devoted)* Love**
Sheri Block Glantz
Cre8ive Writes, LLC

Published by Cre8ive Writes, LLC, St. Louis, MO
Copyright ©2018 Sheri Block Glantz
All rights reserved.

No part of this publication may be reproduced, stored in a retrieval system, or transmitted in any form or by any means, electronic, mechanical, photocopying, recording, scanning, or otherwise, except as permitted under
Section 107 or 108 of the 1976 United States Copyright Act, without the prior written permission of the Publisher. Requests to the Publisher for permission should be addressed to Permissions Department, Publishing Company Name and contact info (usually an email address).

Limit of Liability/Disclaimer of Warranty: While the publisher and author have used their best efforts in preparing this book, they make no representations or warranties with respect to the accuracy or completeness of the contents of this book and specifically disclaim any implied warranties of merchantability or fitness for a particular purpose. No warranty may be created or extended by sales representatives or written sales materials. The advice and strategies contained herein may not be suitable for your situation. You should consult with a professional where appropriate. Neither the publisher nor author shall be liable for any loss of profit or any other commercial damages, including but not limited to special, incidental, consequential, or other damages.

Names, characters, businesses, places, events and incidents are either the products of the author's imagination
or used in a fictitious manner. Any resemblance to actual persons, living or dead, or actual events is purely
coincidental.

Sheri Block Glantz
G.I.F.T.E.D.: (Guiding Ideals For True, Enduring, and Devoted) Love
ISBN: 978-1-7328130-0-7

Library of Congress Subject Headings:

    1. FAM 029000 Love & Romance
    2. SEL021000 SELF-HELP / Motivational & Inspirational
    3. PSY017000 PSYCHOLOGY / Interpersonal Relations

Copyright, ©2018

ATTENTION CORPORATIONS, UNIVERSITIES, COLLEGES AND PROFESSIONAL ORGANIZATIONS: Quantity discounts are available on bulk purchases of this book for educational, gift purposes, or as premiums for increasing magazine subscriptions or renewals. Special books or book excerpts can also be created to fit specific needs. For information, please contact Sheri@cre8ivewrites.com

For those who have taught me what love is (and *isn't*), and those with whom I have shared the lessons.

"Love is not measured by how many times you touch each other, but by how many times you reach each other."
— *Cathy Morancy*

Love can be a noun as well as a verb; a feeling as well as a concept; and given as well as received.

True, enduring, and devoted love is often elusive,
yet continuously pursued. We aspire to it with a sweetheart, reflect on it during heartbreak, and yearn for it with every heartbeat.

Each of us loves or wants to be loved differently — a fact that is vital to any healthy, fulfilling relationship.

Ideally, the words that follow will provide
insight, initiative, and inspiration to highlight
all that you believed love would be...with the people most important in your life.

True, enduring, and devoted love is….

making promises
you can keep.....

...and keeping
the promises that
you make.

wanting each other's happiness.

celebrating each other's successes.

encouraging each other's dreams.

learning to ask for what you need in a relationship.

listening to and striving to meet the needs of the other person.

finding the adventure in life's journey.

understanding each other's *silence*
as well as each other's *words*.

speaking with kindness and respect,
even in the midst of a conflict.

knowing that there will be times
you must put the wants and needs
of your loved one above your own
and having the confidence
that he or she will do the same.

accepting imperfections as part of what makes each other unique and special.

appreciating the good things.

shared goals and vision for what you want in life and in a relationship.

BE GRATEFUL
NOTHING IS WORTH MORE THAN THIS DAY
KEEP YOUR PROMISES
LAUGH OUT LOUD
BE SILLY
BE HAPPY
FOLLOW YOUR HEART
JUST BREATHE
CREATE YOUR OWN HAPPINESS
TRY
COUNT YOUR BLESSINGS

compromising your *wants*, but not your *values*.

the comfort of knowing that disagreements are normal, healthy *and* solvable.

seeking the rainbow after the storm.

ensuring that your actions reflect
the depth of your feelings.

knowing that you can face joy,
sorrow, laughter, tears, and
life's uncertainties...side by side.

the ability to apologize.

the ability to accept an apology.

looking at the "big picture" rather than relying on a small snapshot.

not fleeting.

understanding the fluidity
in a relationship.

not giving up *who* you are,
but rather,

adding another *dimension* to your life.

continually evolve.

wanting to be the best
   version of yourself.

      bringing out the best
         in the other person.

realizing that genuine beauty is
timeless and emanates from the
warmth and gratitude that is
carried in one's heart.

having the fortitude and resolve
to stay the course
because you believe
in each other.

touching a hand
but holding a heart.

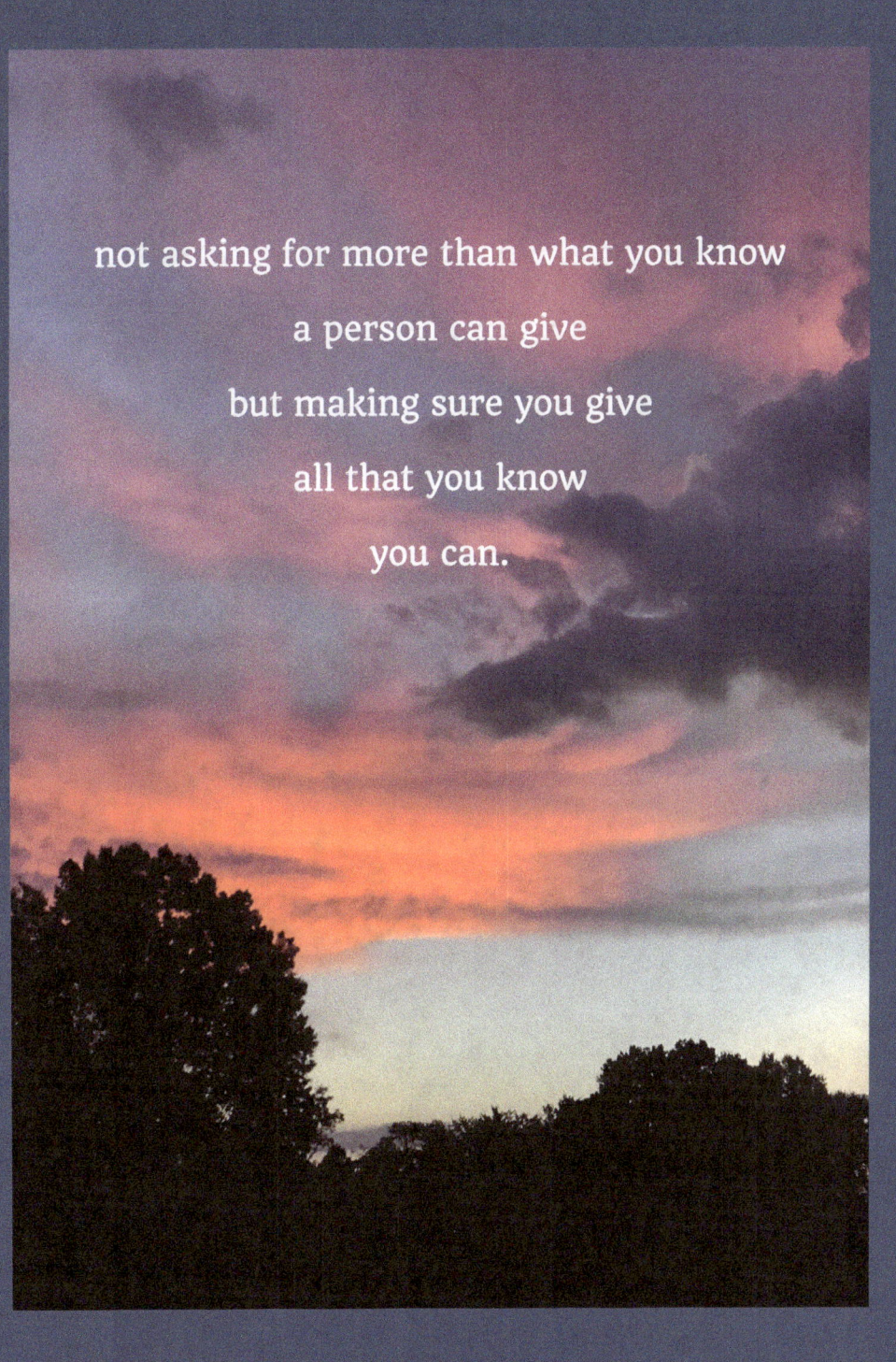

is one of the greatest gifts

that you will ever give or receive.

As a public figure in her community and a lifelong writer, Sheri Glantz, M.Ed., has a unique perspective on life:

* There is always a silver lining.

* There is no such thing as "can't".

* People, circumstances, and challenges are put in our paths for reasons that we will eventually come to understand.

Her versatile talent has been sought to compose works that entertain, explain, and reflect others' sentiments when words escape them. Inspired by life, love, hope, and the continued desire to find meaning and authenticity in her world, she is delighted to share her insights with the public.

To contact Sheri, email her at Sheri@cre8ivewrites.com

www.ingramcontent.com/pod-product-compliance
Lightning Source LLC
Chambersburg PA
CBHW052045070526
44584CB00018B/2618